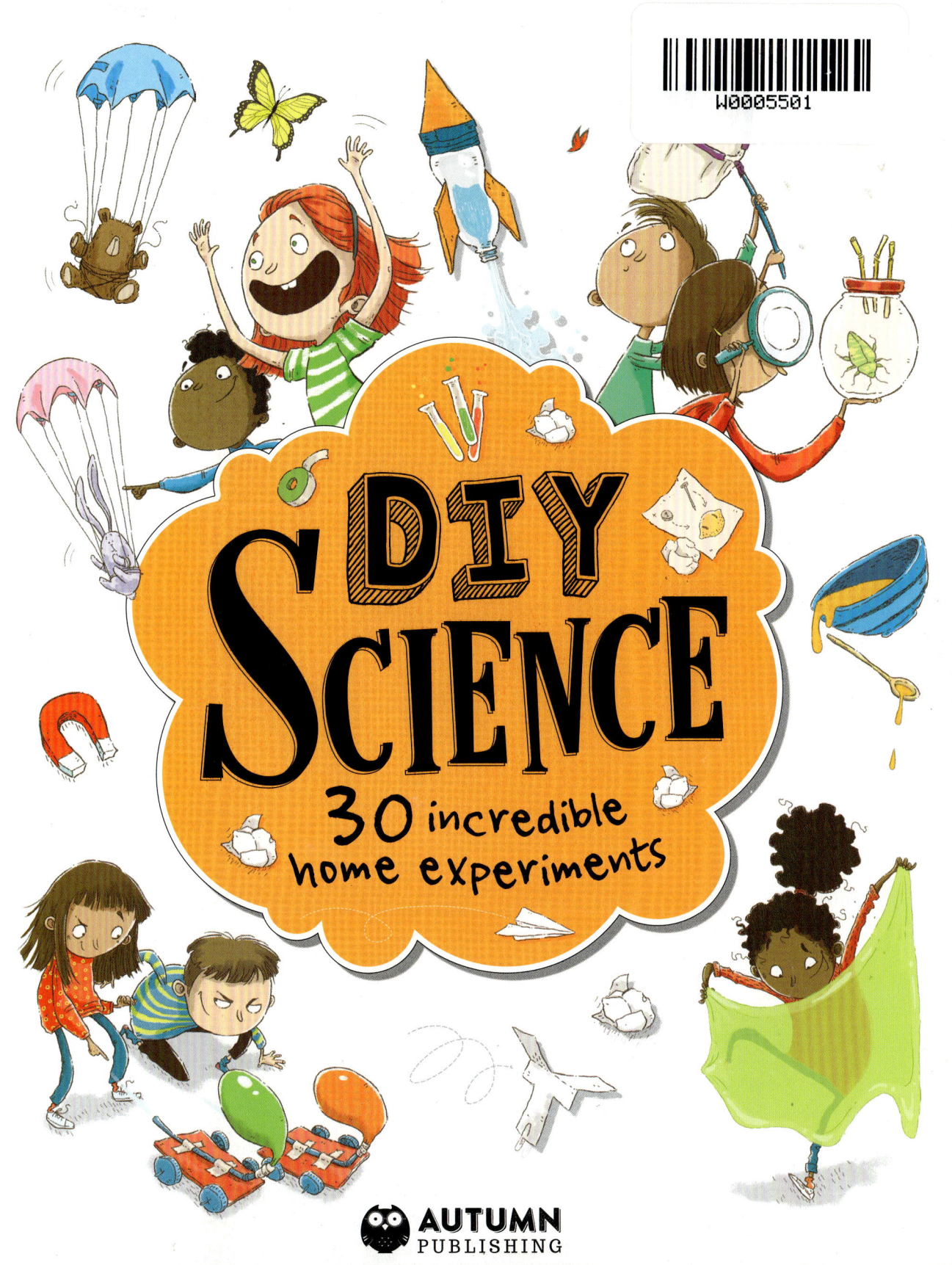

AUTUMN
PUBLISHING

Illustrated by Teemu Juhani
Written by Marnie Willow
Designed by Chris Stanley
Edited by Helen Catt

Additional imagery © iStock / Getty images

Copyright © 2018 Igloo Books Ltd

An imprint of Igloo Books Group,
part of Bonnier Books UK
bonnierbooks.co.uk

Published in 2021
by Igloo Books Ltd, Cottage Farm
Sywell, NN6 0BJ
All rights reserved, including the right of reproduction
in whole or in part in any form.

Manufactured in China. 0721 001
10 9 8 7 6 5 4 3 2 1

Library of Congress Cataloging-in-Publication
Data is available upon request.

ISBN 978-1-80108-750-6
autumnpublishing.co.uk
bonnierbooks.co.uk

CONTENTS

How to be a scientist · 4

Physics
- Bottle Rocket · 8
- Solar Oven · 10
- Marshmallow Catapult · 12
- The Light Fantastic · 14
- Balloon Car Racing · 16
- Toy Parachute · 18
- Fly a Kite · 20
- Static Magic · 22
- Spooky Lemon Light-up Mask · 24

Biology
- Sweeping for Creepies · 28
- Jungle in a Jar · 30
- Hôtel des Bugs · 32
- Caterpillar Nursery · 34
- Beastly Yeast · 36
- Living Cake · 38
- Magic Beans · 40
- Build a Wormery · 42

Chemistry
- Red Cabbage Blue Cabbage · 46
- Giant Bubbles · 48
- Volcano Mania · 50
- Invisible Ink · 52
- Lava Lamp · 53
- Sugar Crystals · 54
- Crystal Geodes · 56
- Unicorn Poop Slime · 58
- Glow-in-the-Dark Super Slimy Slime · 60
- Gummy Goo · 62
- Slime Olympics · 64

HOW TO BE A SCIENTIST

It's helpful to have a notebook or journal where you can write down your notes and thoughts about the world and your experiments.

OBSERVE

Take your science notebook out with you and take notes on things that you see. If you go on a nature walk, write down or draw different birds, bugs, or animals you spot. Keep an eye out for fossils in rocks, or look for shooting stars in the sky. The more you notice about the world around you, the more you'll be able to think of new questions.

ASK QUESTIONS

Why are bubbles round? What makes rockets fly? Keep thinking of questions and writing them down. If you find out the answer later, you can always add that to your notebook, too!

TRY TO GUESS WHAT WILL HAPPEN (BEFORE IT HAPPENS)

This is called making a prediction. What will happen if you try to use a square hole to blow a square bubble? What will happen if you change the shape of the rocket? Write down what you think will happen before you do the experiment.

DO THE EXPERIMENT

Make notes on how you do the experiment. All sorts of things can make a difference to the results. Is it hot or cold that day? Wet or dry? Did you change the experiment in any way? Then write down what happened. If you took any measurements, write them down. Draw pictures or take photos to tape into your notebook.

COME UP WITH NEW QUESTIONS

Use the results to think up other questions. How would you do things differently next time? What do you think would change? Start the process all over again!

This process is known as the **scientific method**. People have been following these steps for over a thousand years, and it has helped scientists work out the answers to questions from "What happens if I hit this thing with a big rock?" to "What shape is the universe?"

NOTES FOR GROWN-UPS

Science is a big topic, so don't worry if you don't know all the answers! If your child asks you something you're not sure about, think together about how you can change the experiment to find out, or where you can look it up.

When doing these experiments with your child, keep things light and fun, and let your child take the lead. Help them with the tricky parts, ask lots of questions, and make sure they stay safe.

⚠ WARNING

Some of the experiments in this book involve potential hazards such as heat or sharp objects. The publisher strongly recommends that parents and guardians supervise their children during ALL activities, giving particular attention to stages marked with a triangle warning sign.

Whenever starting out on one of these experiments, always read through the instructions and consider what safety precautions are necessary. It is a good idea to involve your child with this discussion: identifying risks and taking sensible precautions is a key part of laboratory life. Talk about questions like whether it would be best to wear protective clothing such as goggles or rubber gloves, and whether it is best to do the experiment inside or outside in a safe place. Always use your judgement and stay safe.

Physics

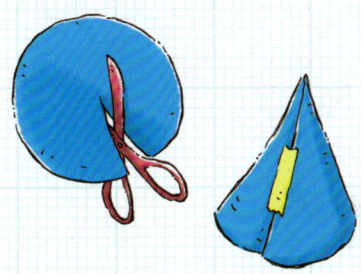

Physics

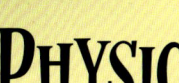

Physics is all about forces, energy, and things that go whiz! Forces push and pull objects. They're what make things move fast or slowly. Energy is stuff like heat, light, movement, and electricity.

Investigate some of the forces you can see in action every day, like gravity, air resistance, friction, and more, by building a whooshy rocket, an awesome parachute, and a whizzy balloon car. Then discover a delicious use for heat energy from the sun and find out how you can get light from a lemon. You'll only sometimes make a mess . . .

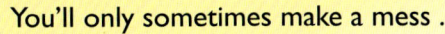

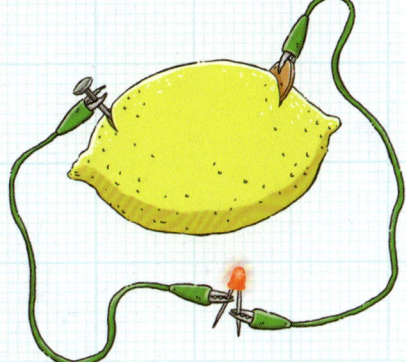

BOTTLE ROCKET

Be prepared! This whooshy, splooshy rocket makes a mess. Get ready to get drenched (and make sure you tell your parents it's all in the name of science).

YOU WILL NEED
- large empty plastic soda bottle
- stiff card stock
- sticky tape
- bottle cork
- bicycle pump with needle attachment
- safety scissors

⚠️ **WARNING** This bottle launches **suddenly** at **high speed** and can travel long distances. Only fire it in a **wide open space** away from people and animals.

STEP 1

Ask an adult to help push the needle of a bicycle pump through a cork. They may have to drill a hole through it first. The cork needs to fit snugly into the bottle.

STEP 2

To make a nose cone, draw a circle on the card stock that is about twice as wide as the base of your bottle. Cut out the circle, then cut a slit to its center. Curve it into a cone that fits snugly over the bottom of the bottle, then tape it in place.

STEP 3

Cut three triangles out of card stock to make fins for your rocket. Use sticky tape to attach them to the bottom of the rocket, sticking out so the rocket can stand up on its end.

STEP 4

Fill the bottle so it's about a third full of water. Plug it with the cork so the needle pokes into the bottle.

STEP 5

Stand your rocket upright, then use the pump to force air into it until it launches!

HOW DOES IT WORK?

Forcing air into the bottle increases the pressure (push) of the air against the water. When the pressure gets too high, the air suddenly pushes the cork out of the bottle. The water sprays downward, which pushes the rocket upward. This is how real rockets work, except they blast out burning hot gas instead of high-pressure water!

WHAT NEXT?

What do you think happens if you use more water? What happens if you use a bigger or smaller bottle?

SOLAR OVEN

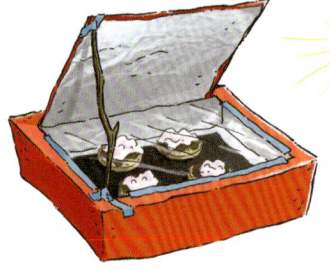

Create deliciously sticky snacks by melting chocolate and marshmallow together using only the awesome power of the sun.

YOU WILL NEED
- empty cereal box
- black card
- aluminium foil
- sharp scissors
- plastic food wrap
- sticky tape
- glue
- stick
- ruler
- snack to cook!

⚠️ WARNING
This oven can get hot enough to burn you. Ask an adult to help you and use oven gloves when handling anything hot. Do not leave unattended. Follow normal food safety rules and do not use the oven to cook raw meat or anything else that carries a risk of food poisoning.

STEP 1
Make sure your box is clean and take out any paper or plastic liners. Then use a ruler to draw a rectangle on the large side of your box, around 1 inch from each edge.

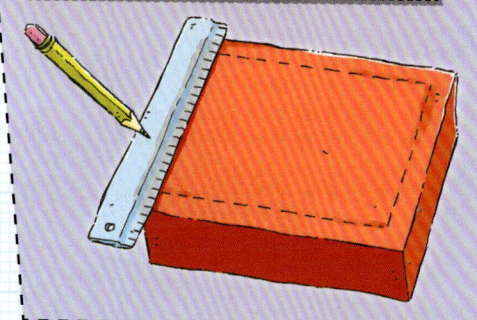

STEP 2
Use scissors to cut out three sides of the rectangle, leaving one side attached to form a hinge. Fold back the rectangle so it opens outward from the box.

STEP 3
Cover the whole of the inside of the box (including the underside of the flap) with aluminium foil. Make sure the shiny side of the foil is showing.

STEP 4

Place a piece of black card on the bottom of the box. Place your snack on top of the black card.

STEP 5

Use a stick to prop up the lid so it stands up straight. Completely cover the opening with plastic wrap, fixing it in place with sticky tape.

HOW DOES IT WORK?

The oven captures heat energy from the sun. The shiny foil reflects sunlight into the oven, while the plastic wrap helps keep heat inside. Hot air rises, so without the plastic wrap, a lot of hot air would just float away. Instead, this air is trapped inside the oven, getting hotter and hotter. This is how greenhouses work!

STEP 6

 Place the solar oven so it faces the sun on a hot day and wait for your snack to melt.

STEP 7

 When it's ready, ask an adult to carefully peel back the plastic wrap to take out the snack!

WHAT NEXT?

Can you change the design of the oven to make it work better? Measure how hot it gets by using a thermometer.

MARSHMALLOW CATAPULT

You can't attack any castles with this catapult, but you can demonstrate the amazing conversion of potential energy into kinetic energy. If that doesn't impress your teacher, nothing will.

YOU WILL NEED
- 4 big marshmallows
- 7 barbecue skewers
- plastic spoon
- sticky tape
- rubber band
- mini marshmallows for ammo

STEP 1
Lay out three skewers in a triangle shape. Put a marshmallow in each corner and carefully push the ends of the skewers into the marshmallows.

STEP 2
Push an extra skewer into the top of each marshmallow to make a pyramid shape. Push the fourth big marshmallow onto the tip of the pyramid to hold it together.

STEP 3
Drape the rubber band over the tip of the pyramid so it sits loosely around the skewers.

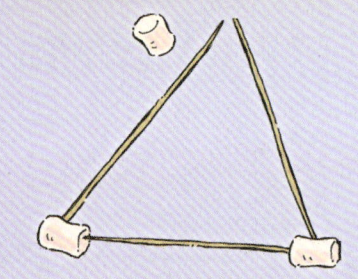
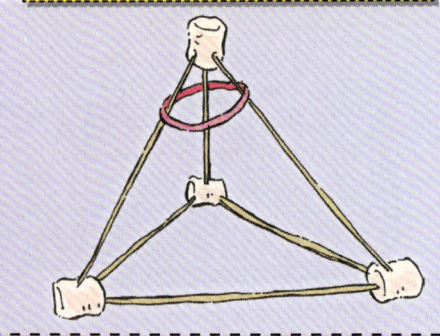

STEP 4

Use sticky tape to attach the plastic spoon to the top of the last skewer.

Top tip!
Your catapult will be stronger if you leave the marshmallows out overnight before you build it.

STEP 5

Feed the last skewer through the rubber band and into the marshmallow in the farthest bottom corner. The skewer should rest on the rubber band.

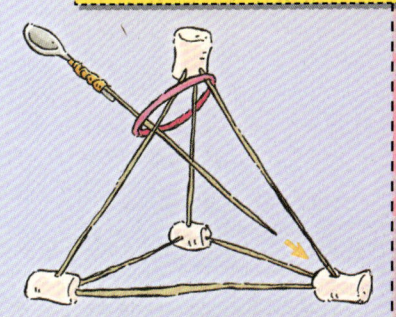

HOW DOES IT WORK?

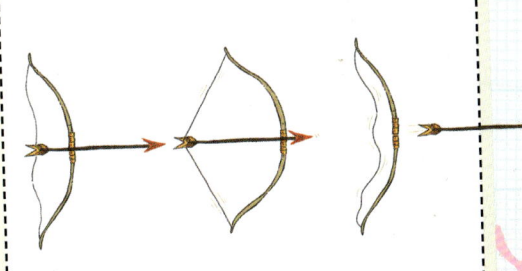

Stretching the rubber band gives it potential energy (a type of energy that has the potential to turn into other types of energy, like heat, light, or movement). When you release the rubber band, the potential energy turns into movement (also called kinetic energy), launching the marshmallow across the room.

STEP 6

Put a mini marshmallow into the spoon. Push the spoon downward so it stretches the rubber band, and release!

WHAT NEXT?

Draw a target on paper and see how accurately you can hit it. Can you think of any ways to change the catapult so you can fire the marshmallows faster and farther?

THE LIGHT FANTASTIC

What color is white light? That may sound like a trick question, but you can find out with this colorful experiment. Scatter light to make your very own indoor rainbow. Pot of gold not included.

YOU WILL NEED
- clear drinking glass
- water
- small mirror
- flashlight
- dark room
- black sticky tape

WARNING
When using the flashlight, avoid looking directly into the light. Ensure the light is switched off before preparation. Do not look directly into the light beam.

Top tip!
The darker the room is, the easier it will be to see your rainbow.

STEP 1

Pour the water into the glass. Place the mirror under the surface of the water. Lean it against the side of the glass so it stands on its edge.

STEP 2

Use black sticky tape to cover most of the flashlight's head, so only a thin strip of light can get through.

STEP 3

Shine the flashlight through the glass at the mirror and look for your rainbow!

HOW DOES IT WORK?

White light is made up of lots of colors. When a ray of light moves between air and water, it bends (refracts). Violet light bends more than red light, so the colors split up and spread out. When the colors reflect (bounce) off the mirror, they spread out even more.

This is how rainbows form in the sky. Millions of tiny water droplets act like the glass and the mirror to refract and reflect sunlight, scattering the colors to make a rainbow.

Prove light is made up of different colors! Take a paper plate and split it into seven sections. Color the sections in the colors of the rainbow: red, orange, yellow, green, blue, indigo, and violet. Push a pencil through the middle of the plate, then spin it like a top. What do you notice?

WHAT NEXT?

Try another mini experiment to see refraction in action. Draw a horizontal arrow on a piece of card stock and look at it through the glass of water. Slowly move the card backward away from the glass. What do you notice?

BALLOON CAR RACING

In this whizzy experiment, you can demonstrate Newton's third law of motion: every action has an equal and opposite reaction. This is just a fancy way of saying if you push your little brother, he pushes back just as hard.

YOU WILL NEED
- cardboard
- scissors
- 2 barbecue skewers
- sticky tack
- balloon
- 2 straight straws
- 1 bendy straw
- sticky tape
- 4 fast-food drinks lids

STEP 1
Cut a rectangle of cardboard to make the base of your car. It should be slightly narrower than the barbecue skewers.

STEP 2
To make the axles, trim the straight straws so they're ¾ inch shorter than the skewers. Thread a skewer through the middle of each straw. Push the drinks lids onto the ends of the skewers and secure them with balls of sticky tack.

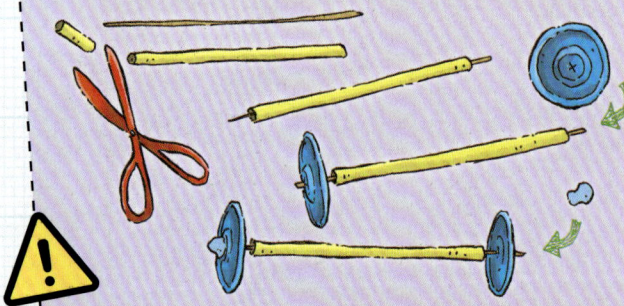

STEP 3
Attach the axles to the base of your car with sticky tape. Make sure the skewers can still move freely inside the straws.

STEP 4

Feed the top of the bendy straw into the balloon. Use sticky tape to create an airtight seal between the balloon and the straw. Attach the straw to the top of the car's base with sticky tape, so the end of the straw sticks out a bit.

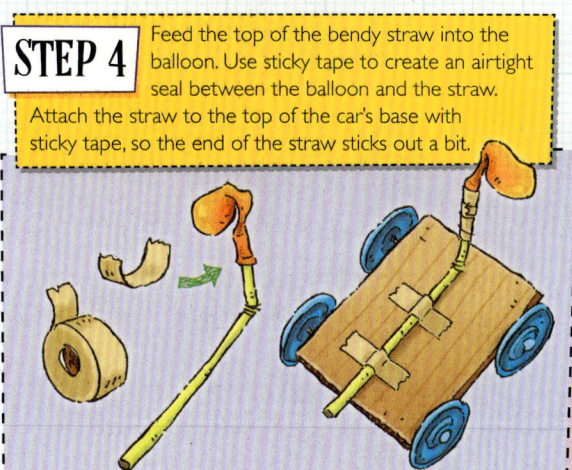

Top tip!
Before you start, blow up the balloon a couple of times and let it go. This makes it easier to blow up when it's attached to your car!

STEP 5

Blow up the balloon. Place the car in starter's position and release!

HOW DOES IT WORK?

When you blow up the balloon, you stretch the elastic by filling it with air at a high pressure. When you release the balloon, the elastic pushes the air back out. The air whooshes backward, pushing the car forward.

WHAT NEXT?

Try making different designs for your race cars. Then set up a racetrack and see which design is fastest. Use a stopwatch to measure their times.

17

TOY PARACHUTE

Is it a bird? Is it a plane? No, it's Pilot Ted making an emergency crash landing. Luckily, with a plastic bag and a yogurt cup, you can make his landing soft as a cloud.

YOU WILL NEED
- large plastic bag
- scissors
- sticky tack
- sharp pencil
- marker
- thread or fishing line
- sticky tape
- empty yogurt cup
- ruler

WARNING
Make sure you drop your parachute from a safe height and in an open place, avoiding dangers of water, traffic, and power lines. Look before releasing to avoid hitting people from above.

STEP 1
Cut along the side and bottom of the plastic bag. Open it up to make a large, flat sheet.

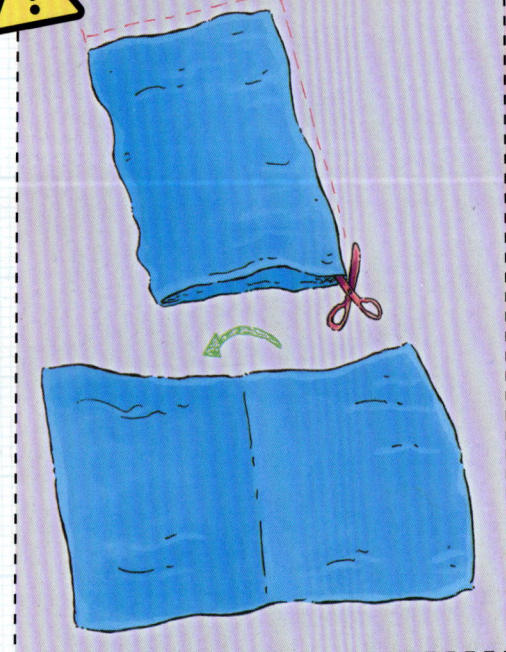

STEP 2
Use the thread to tie the pencil and the marker together, 8 inches apart. Pierce the plastic sheet with the pencil and use sticky tack to hold it in place. Keep the thread taut to draw a circle with the marker. Carefully cut out the circle.

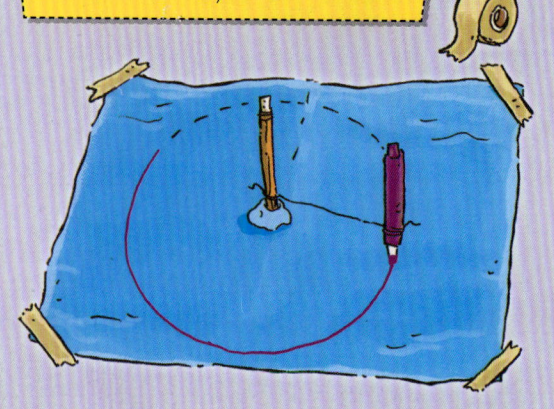

STEP 3

Measure eight pieces of thread 12 inches long. Pierce eight holes around the edge of the circle. Tie a piece of thread through each hole. Use sticky tape to secure and strengthen the places where the string joins.

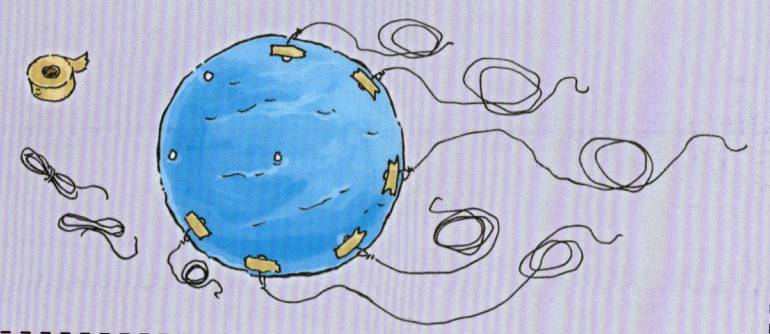

STEP 4

Pierce four holes in your yogurt cup. Into each hole, tie two of the threads from the parachute. The cup should hang like a hot air balloon basket.

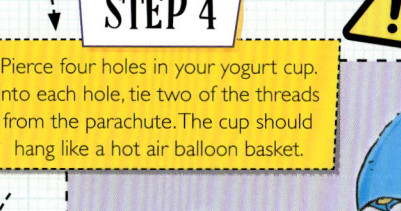

HOW DOES IT WORK?

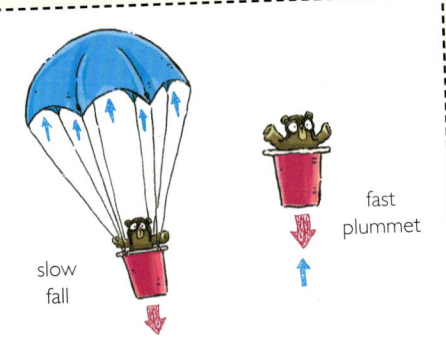

slow fall

fast plummet

Objects accelerate (speed up) when the forces pulling or pushing in one direction are stronger than the forces pulling or pushing in the other direction. When you drop Pilot Ted, gravity pulls him down toward the ground, while air resistance pushes up against him. A parachute increases the area that the air pushes against. This increases the force of the air resistance and stops Ted from speeding up as much, giving him a gentle landing.

STEP 5

Put your toy in the yogurt cup. Take the parachute to a high, safe place and drop!

WHAT NEXT?

Try making parachutes in different shapes and sizes. Which works best? Can you make a parachute that works well enough that you can drop an egg without it cracking?

FLY A KITE

How does something fly when it's heavier than air? It's all due to a force called lift. Helicopters, airplanes, and kites all rely on it to fly. Make a kite to investigate.

> ⚠️ **WARNING**
> Only fly your kite in open spaces away from moving objects and cars, trees, and overhead power lines. Do not use in high winds, or allow the string to be drawn through your hands at speed. Release slowly, keeping the line tight.

YOU WILL NEED
- stiff wrapping paper
- 2 long, thin wooden (dowling) rods
- thin string
- scissors
- ribbons
- sticky tape

STEP 1
Ask an adult to saw the wooden rods so one is 36 inches long and the other is 20 inches long. Ask them to saw grooves or slits into the flat edges at the ends of the rods.

STEP 2
Cross the wooden rods over each other and tie tightly in place, making an "X" shape with the string.

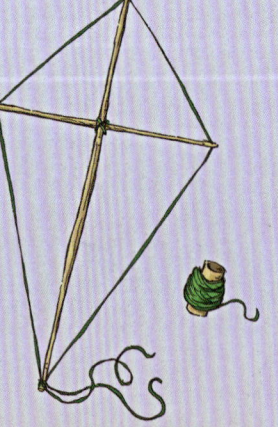

STEP 3
Tie string around the bottom of the frame, leaving 12 inches loose. Pull the string taut around the frame, feeding it through the slits on the ends of the rods. Tie the string tightly at the bottom, leaving another 12 inches free.

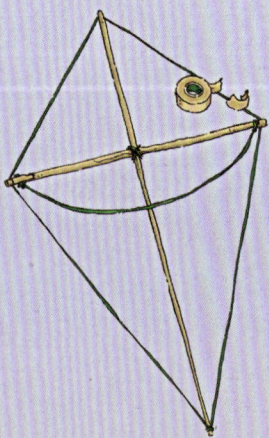

STEP 4
Cut a piece of string 20 inches long. Tie it to either end of the short rod. You can wrap some sticky tape over the knot to keep it in place.

STEP 5 ⚠️

Place the kite frame on the wrapping paper. Draw around the string outline, adding about ¾ inch extra all the way around. Cut out your kite shape, making sure you don't cut the loose strings.

STEP 6

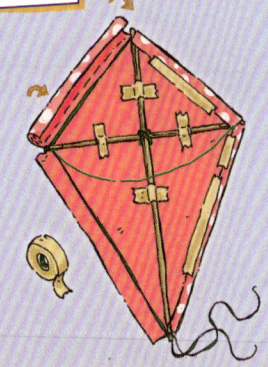

Glue or tape the frame in place on the paper. Fold the paper over the string, using sticky tape to hold it in place.

STEP 7

Take the string that you tied across the horizontal bar of the kite frame. Loop the end of the ball of string around its middle and tie tightly.

STEP 8

Tie the ribbons to the strings at the bottom of the kite to make a tail. Take your kite to a safe place outside to fly it! ⚠️

HOW DOES IT WORK?

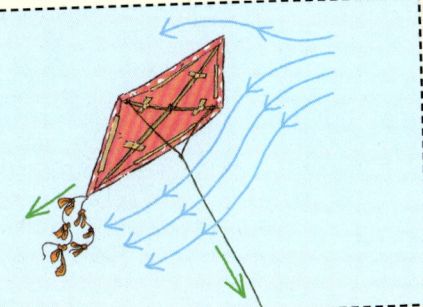

The shape of the kite means most of the wind moves underneath it, pushing the kite upward. This push is the force called lift. The pull of the string downward is equal to the push of the lift upward, so the forces are balanced and the kite stays in the same place. The kite's tail also pulls downward, so the kite stays steady and doesn't spin.

WHAT NEXT?

Does running with the kite help it fly? What happens if you change the length of the kite's tail? What happens if you try to fly the kite with no tail at all?

STATIC MAGIC

You can see static in action in a thunder storm. Negative electrical charge builds up in the clouds until it zaps down to the ground as lightning. This is a huge-scale version of what happens when you rub your feet on carpet, then touch someone and give them an electric shock. Zap!

YOU WILL NEED
- tinsel
- PVC pipe
- wool or silk cloth
- polystyrene plates
- tissue paper
- balloons

⚠ WARNING
Children under eight years old can choke or suffocate on uninflated or broken balloons. Adult supervision required. Keep uninflated balloons from children. Discard broken balloons at once.

STEP 1
Use very thin tinsel (about 1.5 mm across works best). Tie 6 strands together at the end. Measure 6 inches along, then tie a second knot, trimming the ends.

STEP 2
Take a piece of PVC pipe and rub it with a cloth to give it charge.

STEP 3
Hold the tinsel ball above the pipe, but don't let them touch! Gently wave the pipe to make the ball hover.

HOVER PLATE

Rub two polystyrene plates with a cloth to give them static charge. Turn one polystyrene plate upside down and try to place the other plate on top. Can you make it hover?

BEND WATER

Charge a balloon by rubbing it against your hair. Turn on a tap so that a thin, steady stream of water comes out. Bring the balloon close to the water (but don't let it touch). Can you make the water bend?

HOW DOES IT WORK?

Static is an electrical charge that can build up on an object. This charge can be positive or negative. Balloons can pick up negative charge when you rub them with a wool or silk cloth. Objects with opposite charges, like the paper and the balloon, are attracted to each other, while objects with the same charge, like the tinsel ball and the PVC pipe, are repelled (pushed away) from each other.

PAPER PIECES

Cut out tiny pieces of tissue paper. Charge a balloon by rubbing it against your hair or a cloth. Hold the balloon above the tissue paper. What happens?

SPOOKY LEMON LIGHT-UP MASK

Terrify your friends and family with this spooky lemon light-up mask. Choose a dark and stormy night for this experiment to give it extra scare factor.

YOU WILL NEED
- 2 lemons
- 2 copper pennies
- 2 small galvanized (zinc) nails
- sharp knife
- 2 small LED bulbs
- 4 wires with crocodile clips
- cardboard

STEP 1
Draw a spooky mask on a piece of cardboard. Ask an adult to cut it out, making sure they cut a couple of small holes for the eyes, just large enough for the LED lights to slot through.

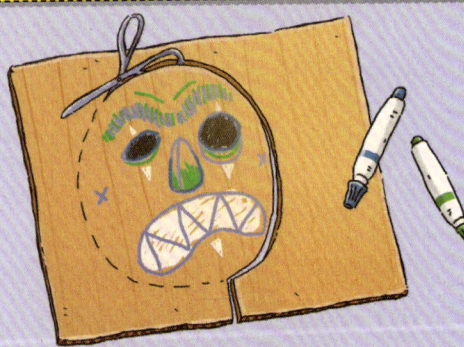

STEP 2
Ask an adult to use the knife to cut two slits through the rind on opposite ends of the lemon.

STEP 3
Put the penny through one of the slits and the nail through the other slit. Make sure the two objects don't touch inside the lemon.

STEP 4
Connect the crocodile clip at the end of one of the wires to the penny. Then connect the other wire to the nail.

HOW DOES IT WORK?

Batteries are made by putting different kinds of metal into an acid. A chemical reaction between the acid and the metals generates electricity. In your circuit, the acid in the lemon juice reacts with the coin and the nail to turn your lemon into a battery. The wires and the bulb complete the circuit and the bulb lights up.

STEP 5
Connect the free ends of both wires to the connectors on the bulb.

STEP 6
Repeat steps 2–5 to make a second circuit, then slot the two glowing lights into the mask. Hide it somewhere spooky and wait for it to give someone a scare!

Biology

Biology is the study of living things. That includes plants and animals (including humans), as well as other living things like yeast and mold.

Lots of biology involves studying living things in their natural habitat, so you'll definitely get muddy doing a lot of these experiments. See what kind of bugs live near you in a park or your garden, then build a bug hotel to encourage new ones to visit. You'll also discover which common garden visitor might one day help humans live on Mars.

SWEEPING FOR CREEPIES

How many creepy crawlies are lurking in the long grass? With a swish of your sweep net, you can discover the tiny world of minibeasts. Just make sure you put all bugs back where you found them!

YOU WILL NEED
- wire coat hanger
- long, straight stick
- old white pillowcase
- strong sticky tape
- shoebox

 WARNING
Don't pick up a minibeast with your hands unless you know what it is. Most creepies are harmless, but some can bite or sting or make you itch.

STEP 1
Stretch out the loop of the coat hanger to make a circle.

 **STEP 2**
Straighten out the hook of the coat hanger, then carefully wrap it around the stick. Use strong tape to stick it in place, making sure to cover the sharp end of the hanger.

STEP 3
Fold the edge of the pillowcase over the circle loop and tape it in place.

STEP 4
Sweep the net slowly through long grass. Then carefully tip the net into your shoebox to see what you've found.

JUNGLE IN A JAR

Terrariums are minihabitats where you control the surroundings to suit your plants. Ferns have been around for millions of years, so they're perfect for creating a Jurassic jungle home for any pet dinosaurs you may have.

YOU WILL NEED
- large jar or bottle
- potting compost
- activated charcoal
- gravel
- small ferns
- moss
- lichen-covered twigs

Top tip! You can buy activated charcoal from garden centers or pet shops.

STEP 1
Pour a layer of gravel into the bottom of the jar, then sprinkle a thin layer of activated charcoal on top of the gravel.

STEP 2
Cover the charcoal with a layer of compost at least 2 inches thick.

STEP 3
Use a small trowel or old wooden spoon to dig a hole in the compost. Gently place your first plant in the hole. Cover the roots with compost and press down lightly to firm it in.

STEP 4
Continue to dig in the plants and moss, arranging them however you want. Add the lichen-covered twigs. If you like, you can decorate your terrarium by adding rocks, pebbles, or plastic toys!

MINI RAINFOREST

Make a rainforest terrarium using tiny bromeliads and polka-dot plants, as well as the ferns and mosses. Keep the terrarium warm in indirect sunlight.

MINI DESERT

Build a desert terrarium using succulents and cacti (be careful handling the cacti). Keep lots of space between the different plants, use a container with a large opening, and keep it in a warm, light, airy place.

TERRARIUM CARE

Keep your terrarium moist, not wet. Spray it with water occasionally. Snip off any dead leaves with scissors and take them out of the terrarium to keep the plants healthy.

HÔTEL DES BUGS

Give your tiny garden visitors a stay to remember with this deluxe bug hotel, filled with only the finest pinecones and rotting wood. It might not be your parents' idea of luxury, but the bugs will love it!

YOU WILL NEED
- old bricks
- ceramic tiles
- roofing felt
- stuff from the garden like pine cones, broken plant pots, cardboard, logs and twigs, dry leaves, bark, hollow plant stems, long sticks, straw

STEP 1
Choose a cool, damp place for your bug hotel. Make sure the ground is firm and fairly flat. Make two sides of a rectangle using eight bricks, four on either side.

STEP 2
Fill the space between the bricks with old logs and straw. Loosely place the tiles on top.

STEP 3
Stack another set of eight bricks on top of the first eight bricks. Fill the space with more garden stuff. Make sure you create lots of nooks and crannies for different creatures to hide in.

STEP 4
Keep adding layers of bricks and garden stuff, using different stuff to fill each layer. When you're done, finish it off with the roofing felt to keep the rain off the insides.

CATERPILLAR NURSERY

Children. They grow up so fast. Only yesterday, you could hear the pitter-patter of dozens of tiny feet and now here they are, ready to fly away and lay their own eggs. Wait, not children. Caterpillars.

YOU WILL NEED
- large plastic tub
- paper towel
- thin hand towel
- caterpillar volunteers
- leaves
- twigs
- paintbrush
- water spray bottle

⚠ WARNING
Look online to identify the caterpillars before you take them away from the plant. Don't take any caterpillars that are rare or that could cause skin irritation if touched.

Top tip! Caterpillars are fussy eaters. Only feed them leaves from the plant you found them on.

STEP 1 — Ask an adult to cut a large hole in the lid of the plastic tub. Leave the outside of the lid intact.

STEP 2 — Line the tub with paper towels and spray lightly with water to make it damp. Add leaves and twigs from the same plant where you found the caterpillars.

STEP 3 — Hold the paintbrush over the caterpillars and let them crawl on, one at a time. Carefully lift the caterpillars into the plastic tub.

STEP 4 — Lay the hand towel over the top of the tub, then firmly press on the lid on top.

HOW DOES IT WORK?

By the time you've found your caterpillar volunteers, they've already hatched from their tiny eggs. Their one job after that is to eat. The more they eat, the faster they grow. When they're big enough, they find a safe place and become a pupa. Inside the hard, protective pupa, their bodies turn into soupy goo that rearranges itself into a butterfly's body shape. When their bodies have completely rebuilt themselves, the pupa peels open and the butterflies emerge, ready to live fulfilling butterfly lives.

CATERPILLAR CARE

1. Make sure the caterpillars have fresh leaves to eat every day. Swap the old paper towel for new every few days.

2. Don't panic if you find caterpillar skins around the box. Caterpillars shed their skin as they grow bigger.

3. When the caterpillars change into pupae, make sure you don't disturb them.

4. When the butterflies emerge, they will need time to let their wings harden before they can fly.

5. When the butterflies are ready, release them outside on a warm, sunny day.

BEASTLY YEAST

Yeast is part of the fungus kingdom, along with molds and mushrooms. In this case, a kingdom is one of the five groups of living things (fungi, plants, animals, bacteria, and protists), not a place ruled by the mushroom king.

YOU WILL NEED
- 3 balloons
- thermometer
- hot water
- ice water
- 3 plastic bottles
- dried yeast
- sugar
- funnel

⚠ WARNING
Warning! Children under eight years can choke or suffocate on uninflated or broken balloons. Adult supervision required. Keep uninflated balloons from children. Discard broken balloons at once.

STEP 1 — Label your three bottles "hot," "warm," and "cold."

STEP 2 — Ask an adult to mix cold and hot water until they have 17 ounces of water that is about 122 °F. Pour this water into the bottle marked "hot."

STEP 3 — Next add 17 ounces of warm water (you should be able to comfortably hold your hand in it) to the bottle labeled "warm." Then pour 17 ounces of ice water into the bottle marked "cold."

STEP 4 — Add 3 spoonfuls of sugar and a spoonful of yeast to each bottle. Swish the bottles gently to help mix in the sugar.

STEP 5

Put the balloons over the tops of the bottles and see what happens.

HOW DOES IT WORK?

Yeast breaks down sugar to get energy that lets it grow and make new yeast cells. This reaction gives off gas (carbon dioxide), which bubbles up and fills the balloon. The warmer the environment, the faster yeast breaks down sugar and the more gas is given off. However, once it gets hotter than body temperature, the yeast cells start to be destroyed and the reaction slows down to a halt.

WHAT NEXT?

Try feeding your yeast different amounts of sugar. Does it make a difference to how quickly the balloons blow up?

LIVING CAKE

Put everything you learned about yeast into practice with this living cake mix. This cake needs looking after, feeding, and keeping warm for a few days. Think of it as your oozy, gooey new pet.

To Start
- 3/4 cup flour
- 1 1/8 cups caster sugar
- 1 packet dried yeast
- 1 cup warm milk
- 1/4 cup water

⚠ WARNING
Ask an adult to handle hot things (including the oven), using oven gloves to avoid burns. Follow normal food safety rules.

STEP 1
Mix the yeast with the warm water. Leave for 10 minutes, then stir.

STEP 2
Add the flour and sugar, then mix thoroughly. Stir the milk in slowly.

SCHEDULE

Look after your cake by following these instructions for nine days. Make sure you observe and make notes on how your cake looks and what changes day by day. Is it bubbly? Is it growing bigger?

DAY 1 — Mix the cake well.

DAY 2 — Mix the cake well.

DAY 3 — The yeast in your cake mix needs feeding. Add ½ cup flour, ½ cup sugar and ¾ cup milk.

DAY 4 — Mix the cake well.

DAY 5 — Mix the cake well.

DAY 6 — Mix the cake well.

DAY 7 — The yeast in your cake mix needs feeding again! Add another ½ cup flour, ½ cup sugar and ¾ cup milk.

DAY 8 — Mix the cake well.

DAY 9 — Your cake should now be ready to bake. Split the mix into four equal portions. Give three to your friends along with a copy of this schedule so they can make their own living cake. Then take the fourth portion and follow the instructions on the next page to bake.

STEP 3
Find a safe home for your cake to live while it grows. It must be somewhere warm and dry where it can be safely left without a lid (cover it loosely with a hand towel). Do not keep it in the fridge!

To Bake

- 1 1/8 cups brown sugar
- 1 1/2 cups plain flour
- 2/3 cup vegetable oil
- 2 eggs
- 1 tsp vanilla essence
- 2 grated cooking apples
- 1/2 cup walnuts
- 2 tsp cinnamon
- 2 tsp baking powder
- 1/4 cup melted butter
- A sprinkling of brown sugar
- 9 inch cake tin

STEP 4 Mix all of your ingredients (except the butter and brown sugar) into a quarter of the living cake mix.

STEP 5 Pour the whole mix into a cake tin, then pour the melted butter over it and sprinkle on the brown sugar.

STEP 6 Bake the cake at 350 °F (180 °C) for 45 minutes, or until the top is golden brown and springs back when pressed lightly—ask an adult to help.

Top tip!
You can experiment with lots of different flavors for your cake. Try pear, chocolate chips, cherries, almonds, raisins, or anything else you like!

MAGIC BEANS

To make a seed germinate and begin to grow, you need **WOW**! That's **W**ater, **O**xygen (air) and **W**armth. Now wow your friends and family with your super science knowledge.

YOU WILL NEED
- dried lima beans
- blotting paper
- jam jar
- scissors

Top tip! Soak the beans for 24 hours first to kickstart germination.

STEP 1 Cut a piece of blotting paper the same height as your jar.

STEP 2 Roll the paper into a cylinder and slide it into the jam jar.

The water makes the hard outer casing of the bean swell up and split. A tiny root grows from the gap.

The root grows downwards and a tiny shoot emerges. They use energy stored inside the seed to grow.

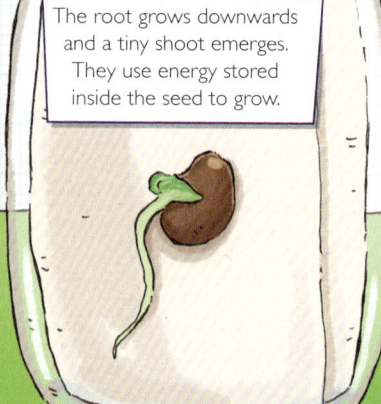

Build a Wormery

Worms are the wriggly cornerstones of entire ecosystems. After studying them for nearly 40 years, Charles Darwin (a famous old scientist) said that life couldn't exist on earth without them. Build a wormery to see why!

You Will Need

- jar with a lid
- sand
- soil
- dead leaves
- worm food
- sticky tape
- worm volunteers
- trowel

STEP 1 Put a thin layer of sand inside the jar. Add a layer of soil on top of the sand. Switch between layers of sand and soil until the jar is about half full.

STEP 2 Add worm food. Dead leaves, vegetable peelings, overripe fruit, and used tea leaves all work well.

STEP 3
Now for the messy bit. Use a trowel to carefully dig for worms in a muddy bit of the garden. This works best after the rain. Carefully place the worms on top of the worm food in the jar.

STEP 4
Ask an adult to poke holes in the jar lid. Leave the jar in a cool, dark place for a few weeks, checking on the worms every few days. Make sure the soil stays damp but not wet.

HOW DOES IT WORK?

Worms are detritovores, which means they eat rubbish like dead leaves and old fruit. As they wriggle underground, they mix trails of broken down plants with the soil. New plants can then take up nutrients (food) from these trails through their roots. Scientists are experimenting to see if earthworms can help make the soil on Mars suitable for growing plants. In the future, worms may be the key to humans living on Mars!

WHAT NEXT?
Test how good your worm compost is. Plant two seedlings in pots, using plain soil for one and using your worm compost for the other (let the worms go first!). Which grows biggest?

Chemistry

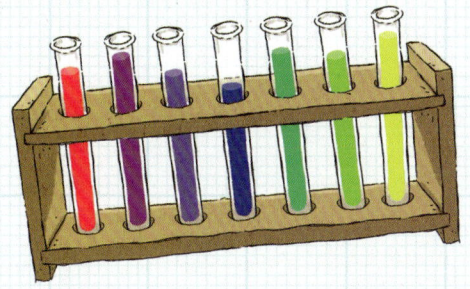

Chemistry

Everything is made out of chemicals. Even you're made out of chemicals. Chemistry is the science of how all those different chemicals behave and how they react with each other. Sometimes those reactions can be pretty explosive!

Find out why slime is slimy, and how crystals grow, and how to make a VERY messy volcano erupt. Is chemistry the squishiest, gooiest, most explosive type of science there is? Maybe. You'll have to try the experiments to know for sure.

RED CABBAGE BLUE CABBAGE

Ahhh, the sweet, cabbage-y smell of science. Amaze your family with this color-changing magic potion. You don't need to tell them that the magic is actually science!

YOU WILL NEED
- ½ red cabbage
- sharp knife
- sieve
- heatproof bowl
- jug
- lemon
- baking soda

WARNING
Take care handling sharp knives and boiling water. Avoid strong acids and alkalis as they can be **corrosive** and **dangerous.**

STEP 1
Ask an adult to help finely chop the red cabbage.

STEP 2

Put the chopped cabbage in the bowl, then ask an adult to pour boiling water to cover the cabbage. Leave the cabbage mix for 15 minutes.

STEP 3
Bash the cabbage with a wooden spoon to release more of the purple color.

STEP 4
Strain the cabbage through a sieve, catching the purple water in a jug.

STEP 5
Take three clear glasses of water. Leave one as pure water. Squeeze some lemon juice into one and mix a teaspoon of baking soda into the other.

STEP 6
Now for the weird part. Pour a little bit of the purple cabbage potion into each glass and see the strange results.

HOW DOES IT WORK?

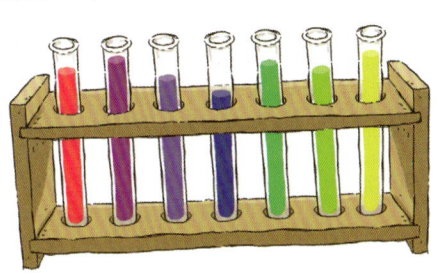

Red cabbage contains a chemical called an indicator. Indicators change color when they come into contact with things that are acidic or alkaline. Acidic liquids include lemon juice and vinegar, while alkaline liquids include soaps and water mixed with baking soda. The more drastic the color change, the stronger the acid or alkali is.

WHAT NEXT?
Ask an adult to help you find liquids around the house that you can test. Can you create a scale of acids and alkalis of different strengths?

GIANT BUBBLES

Get ready to blow some epic-sized bubbles. Prepare your bubble mix the night before if you want your bubbles to be truly huge.

YOU WILL NEED
- dish soap
- glycerin
- water
- 2 long wooden rods
- string (bakers' twine works best!)
- washer
- screw eyes (from a hardware store)

STEP 1
Find a large, shallow container and fill it between 2–4 inches deep with water.

STEP 2
Add dish soap to the water. There should be about three times as much water as there is dish soap. Mix gently.

STEP 3
Add a couple of teaspoons of glycerin. This is optional, but helps your bubbles be extra strong.

STEP 4
To make your bubble wand, ask an adult to screw the screw eyes into the tops of the wooden rods.

STEP 5
Cut two lengths of string, one 20 inches and the other 40 inches long. Then thread the washer onto the longer string.

STEP 6
Tie both strings to the screw eyes on the ends of the wooden rods.

STEP 7
Hold the two wooden rods together and dip them into the bubble mix so the string is soaked through. Carefully lift the string out of the bubble mix, separating the wooden rods, and wave the wands gently.

HOW DOES IT WORK?
Bubbles are like balloons made of soapy water inside. You can't make bubbles out of plain water by blowing through it — they're small and burst quickly. Adding soap changes how stretchy the surface of the water is, meaning you can make bigger, longer-lasting bubbles. The air inside the bubble pushes outward, while the elastic soapy water pulls inward (just like the rubber of a balloon). This elasticity is called surface tension, and is the reason why bubbles are round.

WHAT NEXT?
Instead of glycerin, try adding different ingredients to the bubble mix, such as baking powder, sugar, or corn syrup. Which makes the biggest or longest-lasting bubbles?

VOLCANO MANIA

If you want to get straight to making things fizz, skip steps 1–4 and make a volcano out of dirt in the garden instead!

YOU WILL NEED
- newspaper
- cardboard
- PVA glue
- plastic bottle
- sand or paint
- baking soda
- vinegar
- dish soap
- red food coloring
- funnel

⚠ WARNING
It is recommended that you build and erupt your volcano in an outside area, easily cleanable and away from stainable or sensitive objects and plants.

STEP 1
First build your volcano. Use the gloopy glue to stick the base of your bottle onto the cardboard.

STEP 2
When the glue on the bottle has dried, make a mixture of 1/3 water to 2/3 gloopy glue. Scrunch up whole pieces of newspaper into balls, and dip them into the glue mixture. Arrange them around the base of the bottle to make a volcano shape.

STEP 3
Tear more newspaper into thin strips. Place them over the scrunched-up newspaper, then brush glue mix over the strips. Make sure you don't cover the top of the bottle!

STEP 4
Sprinkle sand over the volcano to make it look realistic, then wait a day for the glue to dry. Alternatively, wait for the glue to dry, then paint your volcano.

STEP 5
Mix together 12 oz of white vinegar, 3 oz of cold water, 1/3 oz of dish soap, and some red food coloring. Use the funnel to pour the mix into the bottle.

STEP 6
Mix 2 tablespoons little bit of water to

STEP 7
Pour the baking soda paste into the bottle, and stand back!

HOW DOES IT WORK?

Your volcano erupts when gas given off by the reaction between vinegar and baking soda reaches a high pressure, causing the liquid to fizz up and out of the volcano. Real life volcanoes work in a similar way, except the high pressure gas is superheated water vapor. This is from ocean water that has seeped through cracks in the Earth's crust into the molten-rock mantle beneath. And instead of red soapy liquid, there's red-hot lava!

VISIBLE INK

This science experiment can be used to send secret messages, making it perfect for top secret spy missions or detecting clues to crack a case.

YOU WILL NEED
- lemon
- paintbrush
- paper
- hair dryer

HOW DOES IT WORK?

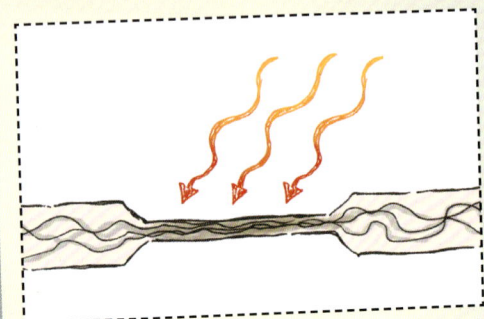

The acid in the lemon juice weakens the paper where it touches it. When you heat the paper, the weaker parts burn and turn brown before the rest of the paper, revealing your secret message!

STEP 1
Cut a lemon in half and squeeze out the juice into a glass.

STEP 2
Use a paintbrush to write your secret message. Don't let anyone peek!

STEP 3
Wait for your message to dry. If you want, you can write another non-secret message in pencil over the top.

STEP 4
Reveal your message by gently heating the paper with a hair dryer or in a warm oven.

WHAT NEXT?
What else can you use to write your secret message? Is there a way to test other liquids to see if they would act the same way as the acidic lemon juice?

LAVA LAMP

Make a groovy lava lamp that's just as perfect for a 70s disco as it is for showing how liquids with different densities behave. Now play that funky music, you coolcat!

YOU WILL NEED
- vegetable oil
- water
- food coloring
- dissolvable fizzy candy
- clear bottle

HOW DOES IT WORK?

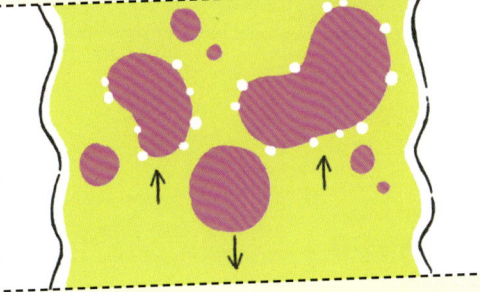

Water and oil don't mix. Water is more dense (heavier) than oil, so it sinks underneath the oil. When the fizzy candy dissolves in the water, it gives off tiny bubbles of gas. These bubbles lift the colored water to the surface. At the surface, the gas inside the bubbles floats away into the air, and the water sinks back down.

STEP 1
Fill a glass three quarters full of vegetable oil, then top it off with water.

STEP 2
Add several drops of food coloring.

STEP 3
Break the candy into small pieces and drop one into the glass. Keep adding the rest of the pieces to keep the bubbles moving!

WHAT NEXT?
What changes if you use warmer water? Does the experiment still work if you put the bottle cap on?

SUGAR CRYSTALS

Grow some colorful crystals. In this experiment, you can eat the results! Who said science couldn't be delicious?

YOU WILL NEED
- hot water
- 2 1/2—6 C sugar
- large heatproof jug
- food coloring
- lollipop sticks
- 4 jars
- 4 clothespins

⚠ WARNING
Always ask an adult to help with handling hot water and glassware.

STEP 1
Ask an adult to pour 13½ oz of boiling water into the heatproof jug.

STEP 2
Slowly add sugar, mixing carefully until no more sugar will dissolve. You might not need all the sugar.

STEP 3
Add a few drops of food coloring to each of the jars.

STEP 4
Carefully pour the sugar water into the jars. Make sure to leave any undissolved grains of sugar at the bottom of the jug.

STEP 5 Dip the lollipop sticks in water then roll them in sugar.

STEP 6 Clip the sticks... cloth... suspended in the... sides or bottoms...

STEP 7 Cover the jars and check on them every day for three days. See how big you can grow the crystals before you take them out to eat!

HOW DOES IT WORK?

A solution is a mix of two chemicals, like sugar dissolved in water. If you keep adding sugar to water, you'll reach a point where no more can dissolve and the mixture is saturated. But if you heat the mixture (adding heat energy), you can dissolve even more sugar, making the solution **supersaturated**. When the solution cools down, it can no longer hold the extra sugar, so sugar crystals form on the lollipop stick. Over time, water evaporates and the solution gets stronger again as there's the same amount of sugar in less water. This excess sugar crystallises and the crystals on the lollipop stick grow.

CRYSTAL GEODES

Geodes are found inside rocks and take millions of years to form. These are a bit quicker, but they're made a similar way and they're just as sparkly!

YOU WILL NEED
- table tennis ball
- gloopy glue
- paintbrush
- alum powder
- food coloring
- heatproof jar
- spoon

WARNING
Always ask an adult to help with handling hot water and glassware.

STEP 1 Ask an adult to cut a table tennis ball in half.

STEP 2 Use a paintbrush to spread glue on the inside of the table tennis ball. Then sprinkle alum powder over the glue and leave to dry.

STEP 3 Mix hot water with alum powder and food coloring. Add the alum powder one spoonful at a time until no more will dissolve.

STEP 4 Cool for half an hour, then use a spoon to plunge the table tennis balls under the surface of the liquid.

STEP 5
Leave the solution overnight, then carefully lift out the geodes. Place them on a piece of paper towel to dry.

HOW DOES IT WORK?

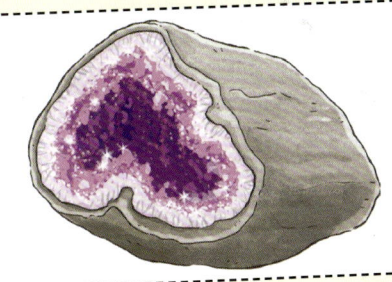

Natural geodes form in air pockets left after bubbly volcanic lava cools and hardens into solid rock. Over time, water trickles through the rocky ground into the air pocket, picking up minerals on the way. When this water seeps out of the air pocket, the minerals are left behind. At first, the minerals form tiny crystals, too small to see. But over millions of years, the crystals grow as more minerals are deposited on top.

WHAT NEXT?
What happens if you leave your geodes in the alum solution for a longer time? What happens if you put the solution in the fridge overnight?

UNICORN POOP SLIME

Unicorn poop slime is a highly scientific substance called a non-Newtonian fluid. Find out more on page 61.

YOU WILL NEED

- 9 oz white PVA glue (school glue)
- 2 tsp baking soda
- food coloring
- vanilla essence for smell
- big squirt of shaving cream
- contact lens solution (make sure it contains boric acid)

STEP 1 Put your glue in a large bowl and add the baking soda. Mix well (it should look a little bit fizzy).

STEP 2 Add a few drops of food coloring and mix it until you're happy with the color. Be careful—if you add too much food coloring, the slime might stain!

GLOW-IN-THE-DARK SUPER SLIMY SLIME

Is this the ooziest, gooiest, stretchiest, slimiest glow-in-the-dark slime you've ever made? There's only one way to find out.

YOU WILL NEED
- 3 1/2 oz clear PVA glue
- 1/4 cup water
- 1 tsp baking soda
- glycerin
- glow-in-the-dark poster paint
- contact lens solution (containing boric acid)

STEP 1 Mix the glue and water really thoroughly in a large bowl.

STEP 2 Add the baking soda, a small squirt of poster paint, and a couple of drops of glycerin. Mix thoroughly.

STEP 3 Add the contact lens solution a little bit at a time. Make sure you've mixed in any clumps of harder slime before adding the next teaspoon of contact lens solution. You may have to use your hands.

STEP 4 When your slime is a stretchy, rubbery consistency, put it in a box with a lid and leave it overnight or until the bubbles disappear and the slime goes clear.

NON-NEWTONIAN FLUIDS
(OR WHY IS SLIME SLIMY?)

Is slime a solid or a liquid? In some ways, it behaves like a liquid. It flows to fill the available space, just like when you pour water into different containers. But it also bounces like a solid. The answer is that slime is a non-Newtonian fluid.

The strange qualities of slime and other non-Newtonian fluids are all to do with their viscosity. This means how fast or slowly they flow. Some liquids are very viscous, meaning they flow slowly, such as honey. Other liquids aren't viscous at all and flow quickly, like water or vegetable oil. Normal (Newtonian) fluids and liquids don't change how viscous they are unless you heat them up or cool them down.

Slime is different. You can change how viscous slime is by the amount of force you use with it. The harder and more quickly you squeeze it, pull it, or twist it, the more viscous it becomes. In fact, it can be so viscous that it behaves like a solid.

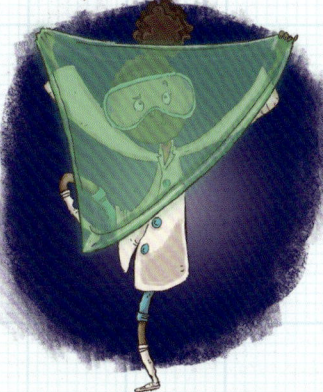

Try pulling the slime apart as quickly as you can.

Then try pulling it very slowly. The slime should slowly stretch and ooze apart. You may even be able to stretch it so thinly that you can see through it.

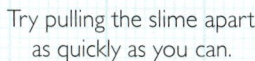

GUMMY GOO

Finally, a slime that tastes as good as it looks. Several gummy bears will have to be sacrificed to make this slime, but it's all for the greater goo.

YOU WILL NEED
- 1 cup gummy bears
- 2 tbsp cornstarch
- 2 tbsp powdered sugar
- 1 tsp vegetable oil
- microwavable bowl

 WARNING Ask an adult to help with handling hot sugar as it can quickly become hot enough to burn you.

 **STEP 1** Ask an adult to melt the gummy bears in the microwave. It should take about 10–20 seconds. Be careful, the sugar can get very hot very fast.

STEP 2 Mix the cornstarch and powdered sugar together, then add it bit by bit into the melted gummy goo.

STEP 3 When it's cool enough to handle, use your hands to knead in the cornstarch and powdered sugar mix. The more you add, the less sticky the slime will be, but if you add too much, the slime will stop being stretchy. Keep going until you're at a consistency you like.